an introduction to

UDC

PROGRAMMED TEXTS IN
LIBRARY AND INFORMATION SCIENCE

An introduction to colon classification
  by C D Batty

An introduction to the Dewey decimal classification
  by C D Batty

An introduction to Sears list of subject headings
  by Philip Corrigan

Learn to use books and libraries
  by T W Burrell

SERIES EDITOR
C D BATTY BA FLA

JEAN M PERREAULT

an introduction to

UDC

ARCHON BOOKS & CLIVE BINGLEY

CONTENTS

PREFACE

The aim of this series of programmed texts in library and information science is to provide instruction in the fundamental techniques of the organisation and use of libraries. The reception of earlier titles suggests that self-instructional media are peculiarly apt for professional education in both a formal and an informal context, and considerable interest has been expressed in the ways in which these texts may be used. Although the first programs were devised as an integral part of a formal curriculum, to be supplemented by other kinds of instruction on other aspects of the subject, they were also used by themselves in practical situations as training manuals for new assistants, particularly in special and college libraries with relatively few professionally trained members of staff. The response of this sector of the profession, in addition to the plan of the series, encouraged the inclusion of a text on the Universal Decimal Classification, and it is with pleasure that we introduce Jean M Perreault's book to the series.

Mr Perreault who has been both teacher and practitioner of library science, and particularly of library classification, is an internationally famous critic and advocate of UDC. He is the author of many papers on the scheme in many of its aspects, and his *Schema* of relators is actively being considered for official use in the scheme itself. This program grew from his discussion and teaching in the graduate library school in the University of Maryland, and more than any other program of its kind in the series so far has received its testing in the practical context of in-service training.

Grateful acknowledgment is here extended to the Fédération International de Documentation and to the Universal Decimal Classification for permission to use examples from the scheme.

C D BATTY
Head of the Department of Information Retrieval Studies
College of Librarianship Wales

INTRODUCTION

The UDC (Universal Decimal Classification) is less well known and less widely used than DC (Dewey's Decimal Classification) or LC (the Library of Congress Classification), at least for organizing books on shelves in libraries. However, UDC is quite widely used in Continental special libraries, often for the organization of classed catalogs instead of books on shelves.

This text will not concern itself with the distinction between the application of classification to books on shelves as against its application to the classed catalog. The only purpose here is to familiarize the student with the powers of this artificial language, and with the problems of translating his analysis of the content of documents into it. Even such closely associated problems as filing order will not be treated except in passing.

UDC, a modification of DC begun around the turn of the century, was intended to be the basis for a universal classification of the growing periodical literature of the day. It attempted to make DC more specific (by giving a greater number of simple subjects) and more concrete (by enabling the creation of complex subjects from simple ones). The organization founded to guide its development is now known as the Fédération Internationale de Documentation; this organization continues to strive to improve UDC in the virtues mentioned, as well as by continuing to make it more truly universal by the elimination of Western bias.

Because of its close relation to DC, it may be helpful to the student to work through either of C D Batty's works, *An introduction to* (the 16th edition of) *the Dewey decimal classification*[1] or *An introduction to the seventeenth edition of the Dewey decimal classification*[2], both in this series. The present text, however, is self-contained, so such preliminary work is not mandatory.

The standard sources of information on the basic phase of UDC (*i e*, the more or less unproblematical aspects represented by the first two-thirds of the exercises) are:

BRITISH STANDARDS INSTITUTION, *Guide to the Universal Decimal Classification (UDC)* (London, author, 1963), 128 pp.

René DUBUC, *La Classification Décimale Universelle (CDU): manuel pratique d'utilisation* (Paris: Gauthier-Villars, 1965), 210 pp.

Peter HERRMANN, *Praktische Anwendung der Dezimalklassifikation*[5] (Leipzig: VEB Bibliographisches Institut, 1965), 111 pp.

Karl FILL, *Einführung in das Wesen der Dezimalklassifikation*[2] (Berlin: Beuth, 1960), 44 pp.

Jack MILLS, *The Universal Decimal Classification* (New Brunswick: Graduate School of Library Service (of) Rutgers University, 1964), 132 pp.

Some of those of interest to the student who wishes to know more about the problems presented in the advanced phase and in the appendix on intercalation are:

T. W. CALESS *and* D B KIRK, 'An application of UDC to machine searching' (*Journal of documentation*, xxiii (1967), pp 298-315); (a technique for indicating all the pairs of correlated elements within a complex code, preparatory to searching a file of such codes stored in a computer).

Robert R FREEMAN *and* Pauline A ATHERTON [*UDC Project Reports* no 1-9] (New York: American Institute of Physics, 1965-68); (another technique for computer searching; many possibilities are explored, particularly that of treating each element of complex codes like a term in a coordinate indexing system).

Jean M PERREAULT, *Towards a theory for UDC* (London: Bingley; Hamden: Archon, 1969), 240 pp; (a collection of seventeen essays ranging from general-theoretic, through structure and notation of UDC, to the question of reclassification).

1*

Jean M PERREAULT *and* J C G WESSELING, *On the Perreault schema of relators and the rules of formation in UDC* (Copenhagen: Danish Centre for Documentation, 1966), [10]+20+26 pp; (on the problem of the indeterminacy of the colon, and on that of citation order).

Cord PETERSEN, 'Zur Problematik von Pluszeichen und Schrägstrich in der DK' (*DK-Mitteilungen*, xi (1966), pp 29-31); (are the + and the / really advantageous?).

Jirí STRANSKÝ, 'Das Kategorienprinzip in der landwirtschaftlichen Klassifikation' (*DK-Mitteilungen*, xi (1966), pp 21-26); (on the problem of citation order).

The exercises that follow are to be done with the classification schedules in hand[3]; even the advanced phase and appendix exercises will not require use of a medium or full edition. You would be wise to read all the introductory matter before beginning the exercises, mainly to familiarize yourself with the vocabulary and the structure of the book. References to the classification schedules will be made thus: p 13 (*i e*, without mention of the work itself).

For those not already familiar with programmed texts, the organization consists of three basic elements: explanations, either preparatory to questions or in comment on answers; questions, for the most part statements of the subject-analysis and form-analysis of a document[4] for which you are to construct an answer in UDC; answer choices. When you have constructed an answer to a question, see if one of the answer-choices corresponds to it; then go to the frame indicated, where you will be told, if the answer is wrong, why it is wrong; if it is right, you will be told how to proceed to the next explanation or question.

Do not waste a great deal of time trying to make absolutely sure of your answer before you see if it is correct; anyone not familiar with UDC will almost certainly make some wrong choices, but the program is designed to help you if you do.

You will be conducted by this program through various difficulties in the use of UDC in the abridged English edition; the general progression will be from simple to complex, and at the same time from familiar to unfamiliar. It is hoped that you will thereby come to see that, even as modest as the schedule-volume appears to be, UDC is capable of being the means for the systematic organization of quite large files of information.

Proceed to frame 1, which begins the basic phase.

[1] (London: Bingley; Hamden: Shoe String, 1965), 94 pp.

[2] (London: Bingley; Hamden: Archon, 1967), 102 pp.

[3] *Universal Decimal Classification, abridged English edition,* 3d ed (London: British Standards Institution, 1961), 254 pp.

[4] The word ' document ' is used for *any* sort of recorded communication, thus including book, map, phonorecord, etc.

EXERCISES—BASIC PHASE

Frame 1

The UDC schedules you are using contain four major parts: a general introduction (pp 5-10) that is a very useful explanation of many features of the scheme; the tables of auxiliaries (pp 10-25) to be used with class numbers from the schedules; the schedules of classes themselves (pp 27-145); and the alphabetical index to the tables and schedules (pp 147-253). We shall begin with simple class numbers from the schedules, and to find them we shall first of all use the alphabetical index; later we shall use the tables of auxiliaries, introducing them gradually. By the time you have finished this book you will have a basic knowledge of where classes and auxiliaries may be found, and how to use them in combination.

If the subject of the document you are classifying is named specifically in the index, then you may turn immediately to the class number that it shows, and check in the schedules that it is appropriate. But frequently this does not happen. If you wish to classify a document on THE HISTORY OF ABYSSINIA, and you look for ABYSSINIA in the index, you will not be given a class number, but a reference to another term. Check this for yourself and then decide what index entry you will look for now.

HISTORY   go to frame 7
ETHIOPIA   go to frame 13
AFRICA   go to frame 5

Frame 2

A place name in the index will often show several numerical codes, for example, as we have seen already,

 ETHIOPIA (63), 916.3, 963

The code in parentheses is for use of the place as a modification or location of another subject. It is never used to represent a subject in itself, and it belongs in the tables of auxiliaries that we shall be using later on. The code beginning 91. . . is for the geography of the place, and the code beginning 96. . . (like any code beginning 93. . ., 94. . . etc to 99. . .) is for the history.

Which code would you use for the document about THE HISTORY OF ABYSSINIA?

916.3 go to frame 6
963 go to frame 11
281.7 go to frame 4
(63) go to frame 10

Frame 3

Yes, 786.6 is the correct translation of THE POSITIV AND THE PORTATIV. You have avoided two possible errors: concluding that because the Positiv (and even less the Portativ) are not as large as modern concert or church organs, that they belong to the family of reed organs and harmonia; and overspecifying by using a code that represents not only the instrument but also its manufacture.

Proceed to frame 14.

Frame 4

No, 281.7 is the entry for the history of the Ethiopian Church, but not for the history of Ethiopia in general. You must have looked at the wrong entry in the index. Be careful.

Return to frame 2 and make another choice.

Frame 5

AFRICA is a place name, so you avoided the error of using the most general available subject; but it is still too broad a term for the place the history is particularly about.

Return to frame 1 and make another choice.

Frame 6

No, 916.3 is the code for GEOGRAPHY OF ETHIOPIA (=Abyssinia).
All codes beginning 91 are geographical.

Return to frame 2 and make another choice.

Frame 7

No, HISTORY is a very general subject; what you need is the history
of one particular place. Always try to look for the most specific term
you can.

Return to frame 1 and make another choice.

Frame 8

Sometimes the terms you use to analyse and describe a document do not appear in the index, and possibly do not appear in the schedule of classes with a specific code. In such cases your own knowledge, or the use of reference works. will give you a more general term to look for in the index, and you may then be able to identify in the class you are directed to some more specific code that will represent the document you are classifying.

If you have to classify a document about THE POSITIV AND PORTATIV you will have difficulty in using the index, since these terms are not listed. Either your own knowledge or reference works will tell you that these are two kinds of organ, and you may then choose a code.

786.7   go to frame 12
681.82 go to frame 16
786.6   go to frame 3

Frame 9

Yes, the codes united by the / are ‘ consecutive ’ in the schedules, in the sense that all the codes between those so united are indicated as well.

Now choose a code for a document about PRACTICAL AND DESCRIPTIVE ASTRONOMY:

522/3   go to frame 23
522/523 go to frame 31
24/522   go to frame 25

Frame 10

No, (63) is the code for ETHIOPIA (=Abyssinia) as a modification of *some other concept,* for example 37 (63) EDUCATION IN ETHIOPIA. We shall come to this later on.

Return to frame 2 and make another choice.

Frame 11

963 is the correct answer. But remember that this is only what the index says, and it is a practical rule that you must *always* check the schedules to make certain you have not misunderstood anything. In this case, when you find the place where 963 ought to be (p 145) you will notice that it is not listed there, though 962 and 967 are. How can you determine that 963 is appropriate?

You will remember that (63) was given in the index for ETHIOPIA as well as 963, so that if we find that (62) and (67) have the same meanings as 962 and 967, then we shall have established a parallel between (62)-and-(67) and 962-and-967, and thus we shall have confirmed 963 as appropriate for ETHIOPIA. The table for place codes in parentheses is on pp 12-21, and the codes (62) and (67) have the same meanings attached to them as 962 and 967. (63) is listed as ETHIOPIA in that table and 963 is appropriate for the HISTORY OF ETHIOPIA. This is confirmed by the note at 960: *"As* (6) ".

Proceed to frame 8.

Frame 12

No, the use of 786.7 for THE POSITIV AND THE PORTATIV is incorrect because it involves an incorrect conclusion about the size of the instruments dealt with.

Check your reference sources again and return to frame 8 and make another choice.

Frame 13

ETHIOPIA is precisely what the reference in the index led you to. A *see*-reference as used here means that the word you have looked under (in this case ABYSSINIA) is not the right place to look, and it will guide you to the term that UDC prefers to use for entry. There is another kind of reference—the *cf* reference—which tells you to compare what can be found under another term, in case it might be a better choice, for example

Perception. *Cf* Intuition.

Now proceed to frame 2.

Frame 14

Now let us look at some of the auxiliaries on pp 10-25.

The first of these is called 'addition and consecutive extension signs', and is used to connect numbers when no single comprehensive code exists for a document. UDC is alone among classifications in allowing for what is called the 'partially comprehensive class' or 'aggregate class' in this way.

To see how this works, first look up the code for PENNSYLVANIA. You are given (748). From this construct a code for a document about THE GEOGRAPHY OF PENNSYLVANIA:

748   go to frame 17
974.8 go to frame 20
917.48 go to frame 22

Frame 15

Now let us look at another auxiliary—the common auxiliary of PLACE, on pp 10-21. You have already seen in the index such place names as PENNSYLVANIA, OHIO, and ETHIOPIA (=Abyssinia); in each such index entry there is given a code in parentheses, and in some are given codes for history and geography of the named place. You have assigned history and geography codes; now you are to use the codes in parentheses as modifications of another subject.

Choose a code for a book about MATERIALS FOR BUILDING CONSTRUCTION IN PERU:

691 (85)   go to frame 18
691+918.5 go to frame 33
68 (85)   go to frame 27

Frame 16

No, 681.82 is an overspecification in that it translates not only THE POSITIV AND THE PORTATIV but also THEIR MANUFACTURE.

Return to frame 8 and make another choice.

Frame 17

Wrong. Removal of the parentheses, changing (748) to 748, entirely changes the meaning of the numerical digits involved; as we have seen already, the note on p 145 implies that if 96 could be divided " *as* (6) ", then the opening parenthesis does not just disappear, as does the closing one, but that the digit ' 9 ' must take its place. (The code you constructed—748—is found on p 138 to mean ARTISTIC GLASS AND CRYSTAL, not PENNSYLVANIA GEOGRAPHY.)

Return to frame 14 and make another choice.

Frame 18

691(85) is the correct translation of MATERIALS FOR BUILDING CON-STRUCTION IN PERU; note that it would also be appropriate for BUILDING MATERIALS IN PERU; USE OF ALL TYPES OF MATERIAL IN PERUVIAN CONSTRUCTION OF BUILDINGS, etc. What is essential is not the words, but rather the ideas represented in them.

Proceed to frame 26.

Frame 19

No, 917.48/.71 (a shorthand way of saying 917.48/917.71, because the first three digits are common to both codes) does give an aggre-gate class uniting the concepts OHIO and PENNSYLVANIA, but since the two codes are not consecutive in the schedules, and since / means 'from . . . to . . ., inclusive', this code means THE GEOGRAPHY OF PENNSYLVANIA, NEW JERSEY, DELAWARE, . . . KENTUCKY, AND OHIO.

Return to frame 22 and make another choice.

Frame 20

No, the code 974.8 means not THE GEOGRAPHY OF PENNSYLVANIA, but THE HISTORY OF PENNSYLVANIA; this can be determined from the facts that 970 is translated as HISTORY OF NORTH AMERICA, and that Pennsylvania is part of North America.

Return to frame 14 and make another choice.

Frame 21

No, there is no meaning of arithmetic division in the sign /.

Return to frame 22 and work through again.

Frame 22

917.48 is the correct code-translation of THE GEOGRAPHY OF PENNSYL-
VANIA, because 91 is GEOGRAPHY, EXPLORATION AND TRAVEL, 917 is
GEOGRAPHY OF NORTH AMERICA, and 917 can be divided as (7) is, so
that 91 extended by (748) drops the parentheses and becomes 917.48.

Now if we classify a document about THE GEOGRAPHY OF OHIO,
the answer by analogy will be 917.71. However, this is all only preparatory to tackling the problem of aggregate classes, and this problem
arises, for example in a document about THE GEOGRAPHY OF PENNSYL-
VANIA AND OHIO.

The symbols for creating an aggregate-class code are + and /. We
use + when the two (or more) codes so united are n o t ' consecutive '
in the schedules, and when any codes listed in the schedules between
the codes so united are n o t appropriate to the document under consideration. We use / when the two (and only two) codes so united
then a l l codes listed in the schedules between the codes so united a r e
appproriate to the document under consideration.

So the code for an aggregate-class document about THE GEOGRAPHY
OF OHIO AND PENNSYLVANIA is

917.48/.71   go to frame 19
917.48+917.71 go to frame 30

Frame 23

Not quite; you are attempting to economize the final code by eliminating the redundant digits, but 522/3 could then be read as either ' everything from 522 to 53, inclusive ', or ' everything from 522 to 3, inclusive '—which last is too baffling to make sense, reinforcing the idea that aggregate classes formed by + or / should have the (numerically) lower code written first. In general you may eliminate redundant digits *only in groups of three*. As you use the schedules you will see examples where UDC has already done this.

Now return to frame 9 and make another choice.

Frame 24

No, the codes united by the / must either be consecutive in the schedules, or all codes between the two united codes must be appropriate to the document being codified.

Return to frame 22 and work through again.

Frame 25

No, you have made two mistakes in choosing 24/522; first, taking the nearest index entry beginning with the word 'practical'; when you did not find PRACTICAL ASTRONOMY, you should have tried ASTRONOMY, where you would have found the subdivision PRACTICAL; second, using the / to unite the two codes, which would mean that everything in classes 24, 25, . . . 29, 3, 4, 51, and 52 up to and including 522 is covered to some extent in this document.

Return to frame 22 and work through again.

Frame 26

Another common auxiliary, that of TIME, using very much the same procedure, will allow you to restrict the period of time covered by a document. The common auxiliaries for time can be found on p 22. Notice that we use a millenium, a century, a decade, or a year as it appears in a date, and we indicate that we mean time by enclosing the digits in inverted commas, ". . .".

Choose a code for a document about 19TH CENTURY AGRICULTURE:

63 "18 "   go to frame 28
631 " 18 "   go to frame 32
631 " 1800 " go to frame 34

Frame 27

No, 69 is less specific than the document requires; check the index again more carefully, and return to frame 15 to make another choice.

Frame 28

You have the auxiliary code right, but not the code for the main class. 63 " 18 " is a code appropriate for a rather more general document, one about 19TH CENTURY AGRICULTURE; FORESTRY, *etc* (as listed at the top of p 104). Examine the schedules and/or the index again and return to frame 26 to make another choice.

Frame 29

Now let us look at a more complex problem.

In the exercises up to now you have dealt either with a simple subject or with a simple subject modified by a simple common auxiliary. Documents will, of course, often present a greater complication than those treated so far, but their translation involves no new principles.

Choose a code for a document about AGRICULTURE IN THE 18TH AND 19TH CENTURIES:

631 " 17 "/631 " 18 " go to frame 35
631 " 17/18 "   go to frame 38

Frame 30

917.48 + 917.71 is the correct translation of THE GEOGRAPHY OF OHIO AND PENNSYLVANIA. Note that the order in which the parts of an aggregate class are stated has no effect on the order of the codes that represent them: see p 10 for the guiding idea, namely that the (numerically) lower code is written first.

The circumstances for use of / in preference to + are:

the codes so united are the beginning and end of a series of codes
   consecutive in the schedules: go to frame 9

the codes so united are modifications of each other, analogous to the
   sign for arithmetic division: go to frame 21

the codes so united are simply consecutive in the schedules:

                                  go to frame 24.

Frame 31

522/523 is the correct code to translate PRACTICAL AND DESCRIPTIVE ASTRONOMY. Note that 917.48/.71 was able to eliminate the redundant digits of its second element by using the decimal point as the signal for the end of the elision; but since 523 has no decimal point, such an economy cannot be attempted, as in 522/3 or 522/23. In general, redundant digits may be eliminated only in groups of three.

Proceed to frame 15.

Frame 32

631 " 18 " is the appropriate code for 19TH CENTURY AGRICULTURE. You will have noticed that the codes for centuries conform not to our way of naming them in English, but to the dates themselves.

Proceed to frame 29.

Frame 33

No, 691 + 918.5 translates a document about BUILDING MATERIALS [not confined to Peruvian use], and about THE GEOGRAPHY OF PERU. Now there may well be a relationship in such a title that would be worth bringing out—if the document were about it. But your document is more general; it is simply about all aspects and types of building materials as they are put to use in Peru.

Return to frame 15 and make another choice.

Frame 34

No, 631 " 1800 " would restrict the period of time covered to the *single year* 1800.

Re-read the instructions on p 22 and return to frame 26 to make another choice.

Frame 35

631 " 17 "/631 " 18 " is an unnecessarily redundant way of stating this subject; besides, it makes the two centuries appear to be more distinct than seems to be implied in the title. If the document thematically concentrated on progress or regress, within the framework of an explicit comparison of the two centuries, the solution would be one so difficult as to challenge the capacity of UDC; we shall examine such cases in the Advanced Phase.

Check frame 38 for the correct answer.

Frame 36

No, 739.1 (32/324) represents the same error shown in the earlier example 917.48/.71, an incorrect code for THE GEOGRAPHY OF PENNSYLVANIA AND OHIO, because it included all the states whose codes lie between .48 and .71.

To review briefly, recall that the circumstances for use of / are that the two codes so united are either consecutive in the schedules, or that if they are not consecutive that a l l codes listed in the schedules between the codes so united a r e appropriate to the document under consideration. The other choice, 739.1(32+354), is therefore the correct one, avoiding as it does the indication of (33), (34) etc.

Proceed to frame 41.

Frame 37

Up to now only simple or aggregate classes from the main schedules, or simple or aggregate common auxiliaries, have been needed to translate the examples. But UDC has other sorts of auxiliaries called 'special auxiliaries', which are not as widely applicable: they can modify only the class to which they are attached, or any part of it. There are often two such auxiliary tables in a class, so two notational symbols are employed to keep them distinct, namely .o . . . and — . . . . These do not *enclose* notations, as (. . .) and " . . . " do, but stand just at the beginning of the auxiliary, like signposts, meaning ' here comes an auxiliary of such a sort '. The special auxiliaries are listed at the beginning of the class to which they are relevant, and they can be used with any code from that class.

Choose a code for a document about MUSICAL FORGERY:

78.061   go to frame 43
78 + 7.061 go to frame 40

Frame 38

631 " 17/ 18 " is the correct translation of AGRICULTURE IN THE 18TH AND 19TH CENTURIES.

A group or series of place names may also occur as modifications of a simple subject, as in AGRICULTURE IN ITALY AND THE IBERIAN PENINSULA, 631 (45/46). Note that whereas places in the m o d e r n world are coded 94/99 or (4)/(9), and that their time-periods, when applicable. are given in the usual codes in quotation marks, places in the a n c i e n t world are coded as 93 or (3). Check p 14 under (3) THE ANCIENT WORLD.

Choose a code for a document about THE ART OF GOLDSMITHING IN ANCIENT EGYPT AND BABYLONIA:

739.1 (32 + 354) go to frame 41
739.1 (32/354)   go to frame 36

Frame 39

Music has only the one special auxiliary .0, but many classes have two; on pp 86-87 you will see the — as well as the .0 special auxiliaries for class 621. Remember that these may be applied only in accordance with instructions. There is no problem with a document about HAND CONTROLS IN MACHINERY, which is —514 when added to 621, giving 621—514. But —514 would be entirely inappropriate for CONTROL OF THE HAND IN PIANISTICS. Nor would a document about VOLTAGE IN ELECTRICAL ENGINEERING, 621.3.015, be a problem. But a problem might arise when both are required at once, as for a document about HAND CONTROL OF VOLTAGE IN ELECTRICAL ENGINEERING.

Choose a code for such a document:

621.3—514.015   go to frame 42
621.3—·514+621.3.015 go to frame 45
621.3.015—514   go to frame 48

Frame 40

No, the code 78+7.061 shows that you rely too much on the index. MUSIC is of course 78, and 7.061 is right for FORGERY, COUNTERFEITING (ART), but you have missed a very important point about the use of special auxiliaries: that special auxiliaries may be used with any code within (subordinate to) the class they apply to.

Return to frame 37 and make another choice.

2

Frame 41

739.1(32 + 354) is the correct translation of THE ART OF GOLDSMITHING IN ANCIENT EGYPT AND BABYLONIA; it would also be correct for THE ANCIENT ART OF GOLDSMITHING IN EGYPT AND BABYLONIA; *etc.*

Documents will probably occur even more often with both a place and a time restriction than with more than one of each. Again the translation involves no new principles.

Choose a code for a document about AGRICULTURE IN WEST VIRGINIA DURING THE GREAT DEPRESSION, 1930-1935:

631 (754) " 193 + 1935 "   go to frame 44
631 (754) " 1930 + 1935 " go to frame 47
631 (754) " 1930/1935 "   go to frame 50

Frame 42

621.3 — 514.015 is not, strictly speaking, incorrect. However, it is not in accordance with the recommended order for combination of a subject and its variously coded special auxiliaries (' citation order '), as explained in §5, pp. 9-10.

After reading these instructions, return to frame 39 to make another choice.

Frame 43

78.061 is the correct translation of MUSICAL FORGERY, even though it is not disclosed in the index, by virtue of the rule that a special auxiliary modifies the class to which it is attached, *or any part of it.* 78 is a part of 7; therefore .061 may modify 78 (and 71, 72, etc).

Proceed to frame 39.

Frame 44

No, there are two errors involved in " 193+1935 "; first, a decade, " 193 ", and a year, " 1935 ", are named together, the one including the other, and to say ' the 1930's as well as 1935 ' is pointless; second, the dash in the original wording intended not a separate pair of times, but a span of time (not shown with +).

Return to frame 41 and make another choice.

Frame 45

No, 621.3—514+621.3.015 as an answer reveals a confusion in your mind about the difference between aggregate classes and complex classes of the sort you are faced with here.

To review briefly, note that a ' literal ' retranslation of your answer would read HAND CONTROL IN ELECTRICAL ENGINEERING; *and* IRRADIATION EQUIPMENT. What is wanted is a code that represents not an *aggregate* of modifications, but a *complex* of modifications; in other words, ask yourself how the various subordinate concepts in the abstract to be translated can be made to modify each other, not merely to modify the principal concept separately.

Return to frame 39 and make another choice.

Frame 46

334 (1—651) is the right translation for THE COOPERATIVE MOVEMENT IN STATES AT WAR. The same technique can apply to particular places, combining subject, place, and place-special-auxiliary.

Choose a code for a document about THE WASPS OF THE UNEXPLORED REGIONS OF LABRADOR:

595.798 (1—08)+(719) go to frame 52
595.798 (719—08)   go to frame 56
595.79 (719—08)   go to frame 59

Frame 47

No, 631 (754) " 1930+1935 " is correct in its translation of AGRICUL-
TURE and of WEST VIRGINIA, but it excludes the years 1931, 1932,
1933 and 1934.

Return to frame 44 and make another choice.

Frame 48

621.3.015—514 is the accepted way to construct the code for HAND
CONTROL OF VOLTAGE IN ELECTRICAL ENGINEERING. The rule in §5,
pp 9-10, does not always give perfect results, but here it is satisfactory,
since the equipment would have to be taken for granted before any
sort of control over it could be effected (this is called by S R Ranga-
nathan the ' wall-picture principle ').

Proceed to frame 51.

Frame 49

No, 334 is correct but (−651) is not allowed because a special auxiliary must be attached to one of the codes in the list it applies to; it can never stand by itself.

Re-read frame 51 and make another choice.

Frame 50

631 (754) " 1930/1935 " is the correct translation of AGRICULTURE IN WEST VIRGINIA DURING THE GREAT DEPRESSION, 1930-1935; you will note, in practical work, that the dates specifying a period of time are often not explicitly mentioned in the document's title, or that the dates used by one author to specify a named period of time do not agree with those used so by another. UDC is unusual in allowing flexibility in the coded statements of such periods; this is another case of the attempt to solve the problem of aggregate classes.

Proceed to frame 37.

Frame 51

It is not only subjects in the main schedules that have special auxiliaries; some common auxiliaries have their own special auxiliaries. One such is the common auxiliary of PLACE. On p 13 you can see these special auxiliaries, given with the introductory symbol — ...., for example (—13) SOUTH.

Such a special auxiliary must always follow some geographical-place code or other, even if only the place (1) that we might call 'any-place'. Check the note on p 13 under (—) ZONES, ORIENTATION, GROUPINGS, SPHERES, *etc*.

Choose a code for a document about THE COOPERATIVE MOVEMENT IN STATES AT WAR:

334 (1—651)   go to frame 46
334 (—651)   go to frame 49
334 (100—651) go to frame 53

Frame 52

No, you have allowed the previous example to make you think that the — special auxiliaries for place never follows anything except the digit ' 1 '. What you must do here is to attach the code (—08) to the code for the place LABRADOR.

Return to frame 46 and make another choice.

Frame 53

No, 334 is correct, but (100—651) is too restrictive, by specifying that a l l places are discussed, whereas we have a document which implies only ' in whichever places . . .'.

Return to frame 51 and make another choice.

Frame 54

In all the cases you have worked through so far, the only sort of modification you have encountered has been that of subordination; and the subordinated concept has been a restriction on what it modifies —it makes it less general. But there are common auxiliaries that modify without restricting the subject; they indicate something purely formal about the book, or about the way the subject is presented. One such is the common auxiliary of FORM, on pp 9-10.

Choose a code for a document arranged according to that fashion commonly called POCKET DICTIONARY, about COSTUME:

391, 03   go to frame 57
391 (033) go to frame 60
39 (03)   go to frame 63

Frame 55

There are other aspects of a book besides its form which may be of value to an inquirer in helping him to decide whether he should attempt to use it—aspects which are similar to form in that they are not anything the book is about. One such aspect is language. Commonly, languages other than the vernacular used in the library for which you are classifying are all that are to be coded. If, however, your library's policy is to code all languages, each of the books you have done up to now would have needed a code showing that it was in English. If you check in the index, you will see that the entry ENGLISH, LANGUAGE has the codes =20 and 420 attached; you should recognize 420 as a main schedule code and =20 as a common anxiliary by the presence of the introductory symbol.

Choose a code for a set of documents about music in general, with the title REVUE MUSICALE (most if not all of the articles in which are in French), which has been issued in that fashion commonly called PERIODICAL:

78 (05)=40   go to frame 62
792.6=40   go to frame 65
78 (048.1)=40 go to frame 68

Frame 56

595.798 (719—08) is the appropriate translation of THE WASPS OF THE UNEXPLORED REGIONS OF LABRADOR. We will return to further subtleties of the common auxiliaries of place later.

Another such common auxiliary with its own special auxiliaries is that for TIME. These are slightly simpler than those for PLACE, since the non-chronological special auxiliaries do not have to be preceded by the chronological ones.

Choose a code for a document about STREET MARKETS IN LIECHTENSTEIN IN THE WINTER-TIME:

381.14 (436.48) " 324 "   go to frame 58
943.648 " 324 "+381.14 go to frame 69
381.14 " 324 " (436.48)   go to frame 64

Frame 57

If you seriously mean this choice, you are not paying the sort of attention you ought to pay; the 391 is correct, but the comma is entirely wrong, since it copies the punctuation separating (03) and 03 in the index.

Return to the very beginning and work through again (if you came to this page just out of curiosity, return to frame 54 and make another choice).

Frame 58

By now there should be no one who makes mistakes about the elementary parts of these codes; but there can be argument about their combination. You have had an example combining a subject, a place, and a period in that order; the translation 381.14 (436.48) "324" for STREET MARKETS IN LIECHTENSTEIN IN THE WINTER-TIME is correct, and follows the instructions in §5, pp 9-10. However, there is much to be said for the choice in frame 64, which gives more emphasis to the time-aspect—which after all may well be a more important aspect in an economic discussion than is mere place. More about such problems of citation order will be discussed in the Advanced Phase.

Proceed to frame 54.

Frame 59

This is not a wrong answer, though the index does not lead to it (the place part is quite correct); but it reflects perhaps an exaggerated caution: you probably chose it in the fear that some of the "wasps" discussed might not qualify zoologically, such as wood-wasps, sand-wasps, and gold-wasps. But this would not be where the index would lead the inquirer.

Return to frame 46 and make another choice.

Frame 60

391 (033) is the correct translation of POCKET DICTIONARY ABOUT COSTUME. Form codes of this sort may be attached to any subject code; an important point to remember in their use is that they are not meant to convey the subject content of the document. Such subject content (for instance if we seek a classification for a book *about* DICTIONARIES) must be found outside the (o . . .) common auxiliary, since a common auxiliary normally serves as a modifier of some other code.

Proceed to frame 55.

Frame 61

No, 943.648 " 324 "+381.14 would be appropriate as a translation of WINTER-TIME HISTORY OF LIECHTENSTEIN, as well as being about STREET MARKETS. If you seriously thought that this answer was possible, you had best return to the very beginning and work through again (if you came to this page just out of curiosity, return to frame 56 and make another choice).

Frame 62

78 (05)=40 is the right choice, representing the general subject MUSIC with two formal modifications: PERIODICAL and IN FRENCH.

Note that another wrong codification would be 78=40 (05), which would retranslate as A PERIODICAL ON MUSIC WRITTEN [!] IN FRENCH. The language-code must follow the form-code if it is to specify it.

Proceed to frame 66.

Frame 63

39 is far too general; perhaps you confused COSTUME and CUSTOMS when you looked in the index. Be more careful from now on, lest sometimes your work may not be corrected and you grow accustomed to slovenliness! (03) is correct as translation of DICTIONARY, but you did not look around, as must always be done, to note that the line below the one indicated in the index carries an instruction about division of (03) in the same way that (02) is divided, and that the next line gives an example of this division that is just what you are looking for: (033), CONCISE, POCKET DICTIONARIES.

Return to frame 54 and make another choice.

Frame 64

381.14 " 324 " (436.48) is not an answer constructed according to the instructions, but it has much to recommend it.

Read frame 58 and then proceed to frame 54.

Frame 65

No, you are wrong, even though the idea of a musical review is one closely enough associated with that of a musical comedy to make this an appropriate translation for a document about that form of entertainment called 'la revue musicale'; but remember that what you are classifying is a periodical with a far more general subject. However, the language code =40 is correct.

Return to frame 55 and make another choice.

Frame 66

Now, to turn to a feature of UDC that is the focus of more criticism, as well as more praise, than any other, you are to learn the use of the colon, which shows relation between codes of the same sort. Occasionally you will find an index entry which explicitly tells you to use a pair of codes with a colon between them, as at ABSORPTION, HEAT 536.3:535.34. However, the advantage to be gained from use of the colon is that it can be used whenever required, often but not always shown by an example, as at 75.05 USES OR APPLICATIONS OF PAINTING; the examples given on p 196 are :096, :792.4, :929.6, which mean (respectively) PAINTING APPLIED TO ILLUSTRATED BOOKS, TO THE MUSICAL THEATER, and TO COATS OF ARMS. Accordingly, painting applied to other subjects can be shown in an analogous way.

Choose a code for a document about COPPER ELECTRIC CONDUCTING MATERIALS:

621.315.5:669   go to frame 69
621.315.5:669.3   go to frame 72
621.315.5:546.56   go to frame 75

Frame 67

No, 295:291.23 is wrong in that you did not check the code you found in the index under ZOROASTRIANISM, 295, against the schedules, violating the rule mentioned in frame 11. Your code means THE ESCHATOLOGICAL DOCTRINE OF THE ZOROASTRIANS, without the essential aspect EARLY.

Return to frame 72 and make another choice.

Frame 68

No, you are depending too heavily on the index for the translation of REVUE; 78 and =40 are correct, but a check of the schedules for (048.1) would have revealed that it means REVIEW in a different sense than PERIODICAL (=review).

Return to frame 55 and make another choice.

Frame 69

No, 621.315.5 : 669 says no more than METALLIC ELECTRIC CONDUCTING MATERIALS; the note " *By* : 669 " means that if it is appropriate, the particular conducting material can be specified by a code of the 669 type.

Return to frame 66 and make another choice.

Frame 70

No, 295.4:236 is wrong in that you found the entry ESCHATOLOGY in the index you simply took the first listed code, violating the rule in frame 11 about always consulting the schedules before assigning a code, which was reinforced in frame 72 by the warning about the appropriate context. The code you chose means RELATION BETWEEN EARLY ZOROASTRIANISM AND THE C H R I S T I A N DOCTRINE OF ESCHATOLOGY.

Return to frame 72 and make another choice.

Frame 71

355.43 (37:38) is the appropriate translation of COMPARISON BETWEEN ANCIENT GREEK AND ROMAN STRATEGY. Another way of saying the same thing would be 355.43 (37):355.43 (38), which avoids the prohibition of colon-relating two codes of different sorts; but though the two sub-entries that result from this way of coding it should in fact both be filed in the catalog, the same double sub-entries can be seen in the less clumsy and redundant way given at the beginning of this paragraph. Remember that you can so relate two time-codes, form-codes, as well as place-codes. Some problems will arise in some such uses; in the Advanced Phase you will get to see some of them.

Proceed to frame 77.

Frame 72

621.315.5:669.3 is the correct choice. Be careful that your choices of related codes, as you have done here, is made with full awareness of the context of the codes being related. Here copper in the metallurgical context is appropriate, while copper in the chemical context is not.

Now you can try a use of the colon where not even examples are given: choose a code for a document about THE ESCHATOLOGICAL DOCTRINE OF THE EARLY ZOROASTRIANS:

295.4:291.23   go to frame 74
295:291.23   go to frame 67
295.4:236   go to frame 70

Frame 73

355.43:937:938 is not, strictly speaking, a mistake, but it is not the accepted way to translate COMPARISON BETWEEN ANCIENT GREEK AND ROMAN MILITARY STRATEGY, largely because it is not the most economical way of doing it, but even more important because MILITARY HISTORY (IN GENERAL) OF ANCIENT GREECE would not involve using 938, but would be 355.48 (38) or 355 (38), depending on the degree of generality.

Return to frame 74 and make another choice.

Frame 74

295.4:291.23 is the appropriate translation of THE ESCHATOLOGICAL DOCTRINE OF THE EARLY ZOROASTRIANS. At the risk of boring you with the same device, note that the colon was mentioned in frame 66 as showing relation between codes of the same sort. This means that you would never have occasion to translate A PERIODICAL ON ECONOMICS as 33:(05), or CHILDREN'S SONGS OF EASTERN ALBANIA as 784.67:(469.5—11). In each case the correct code would be obtained just by dropping the colon, since the relationship is already shown by subordinating signs like (o . . .) and (. . .). Thus we come by a back door to an earlier point: the colon is only used between codes of the same sort—it is not *subordinating* but *coordinating*.

Accordingly, it can be used for more than just the conjunction of codes from the main schedules. Choose a code for a document about COMPARISON BETWEEN ANCIENT GREEK AND ROMAN MILITARY STRATEGY:

355.43(37:38)   go to frame 71
355.43:937:938 go to frame 73
355.43:(37):(38) go to frame 76

Frame 75

No; while 621.315.5 is correct, colon-relation of it to the code you have found in the index would be inappropriate, since 546.56 means THE CHEMISTRY OF COPPER, not THE METALLURGY OF COPPER, which after all is the sort of context needed for the document being classified.

Return to frame 66 and make another choice.

Frame 76

No, 355.43:(37):(38) violates the prohibition, given in frame 74, of joining two different sorts of code with the colon—and you chose to do just that.

Return to frame 74 and make another choice.

Frame 77

Another common auxiliary that is a source of criticism, and of rather less praise, is that of POINT OF VIEW. An auxiliary of this sort is normally taken to be somewhere between the true subject modifiers like place, time, or special auxiliaries, and the form or language auxiliaries which have no effect at all on subject content. This point of view auxiliary is widely used for the organization of commercial correspondence files, quite independent of UDC itself. Another widespread application of the point-of-view common auxiliaries (and one better integrated with UDC itself) is that of providing an alternative way of dividing up any main class, especially when other main classes are to be coloned on; see the example on p 23.

Choose a code for a document about PHARMACOLOGISTS:

615.5.009.5   go to frame 81
615.5.007.1   go to frame 83
615.53—05   go to frame 88
615.5:331.713 go to frame 85

Frame 78

Choose a code for a document about EMIGRATION FROM POLAND OF GERMAN-SPEAKING JEWS DURING THE PERIOD BETWEEN WORLD WARS I AND II:

325.252 (=924) " 1919/1939 "   go to frame 82
94/99 (=924=30) (438) " 1919/1939 " go to frame 84
325.252 (438)=30   go to frame 86
325.252 (438) (=924=30) " 1919/1939" go to frame 89

Frame 79

As was implied by the rule ' Normally use a special auxiliary in preference to a common auxiliary, and normally use an auxiliary in preference to a coloned code ', there are cases where the same meaning can be achieved in a variety of codifications. But if the meaning is different in some cases, the rule does not apply. Your problem, therefore, is to notice when the meaning is the same and when it differs.

Proceed to frame 80.

Frame 80

A case where the meaning is definitely different is involved in forms when they are used as topics. You will notice on p 28 that class 04 has the note "*As* (04)", which means that there is a total parallelism between the two schedules. Why then have two schedules at all? (04) is used as a modification of some subject, as 322(42)(04) ESSAYS, BROCHURES, ADDRESSES, ETC ON CHURCH AND STATE IN ENGLAND. Is 04 then the code for ESSAYS, BROCHURES, ADDRESSES ON EVERYTHING IMAGINABLE? Though in fact this is the use to which it is often put, 04 should be reserved to translate the s u b j e c t ESSAYS, BROCHURES, ADDRESSES, ETC. Thus a book about DOCUMENTATION which is in fact a bundle of essays, brochures, addresses, etc. bound up together, is coded 002(04), whereas one about DOCUMENTATION OF COLLECTION OF ESSAYS, BROCHURES, ADDRESSES, ETC is coded 04:002.

Choose a code for a set of documents about PERIODICALS IN UNIVERSITY LIBRARIES, which has been issued in that fashion commonly called PERIODICAL:

027.7:05   go to frame 90
027.7 (05) (05) go to frame 87
027.7:05 (05) go to frame 93

Frame 81

No, 615.5.009.5 is inappropriate to translate PHARMACOLOGISTS, because though 615.5 translates PHARMACY, .009.5 is simply the earliest occurrence of a common point-of-view among the index entries beginning PERSONAL, and represents when the schedules are consulted, a wholly erroneous concept. What you need is a way of saying PHARMACY—ITS PROFESSIONAL PRACTITIONERS.

Return to frame 77 and make another choice.

Frame 82

94/99 (=924=30) (438) " 1919/1939 " represents a grasping at straws. If you had a general book about HISTORY OF THE JEWS SINCE THE MIDDLE AGES, 94/99 (=924) would do, and other modifications could of course be added on. But there is one element that you have wholly ignored in choosing this code, an element which is more important than all the rest.

Return to frame 78 and make another choice.

Frame 83

615.5.007.1 is the appropriate translation of PHARMACOLOGISTS (= professionals in the field of pharmacy); this demonstrates the most legitimate use of the common point-of-view auxiliary, one that depends neither on isolation from UDC (as in correspondence files) nor on the desire to impose a different filing order on coloned-on codes. But you will have noted that in this use it becomes something more concrete than just a point of view, and almost a subject modification.

Since the publication of the English third abridged edition, the —05 auxiliary, previously restricted to class 3, has been made available throughout, giving 615.5—05 as the correct translation of PHARMACOLOGISTS; such an answer was not proposed as a choice above, though, since you would have had to reject as unauthorized by your authority document—namely by the third abridged edition.

The last of the common subject-modifying auxiliaries is that for race or nationality, shown by combination of language and place notations, as (= . . .). Thus a book about TECHNOLOGY OF THE GERMANIC RACES is coded 62 (=3), and one about TECHNOLOGY AMONG THE ANCIENT AMERICAN INDIANS is coded 62 (=1.399). This latter example demonstrates how the examples on p 21 can be expanded, and how there are borrowings of place codes to prevent a whole new place schedules having to be costructed to specify races. Similarly, a book about TECHNOLOGY AMONG THE FRENCH-SPEAKING MODERN AFRICAN RACES is coded as 62 (=96=40), one about TECHNO-LOGY AMONG ITALIAN-SPEAKING AMERICANS as 62 (=1.73=50).

Proceed to frame 78.

Frame 84

325.252 (438) is correct, though the terminal element =30 must be interpreted only as indicating the language of the document. But you have ignored the very important elements JEWS and DURING THE PERIOD BETWEEN WORLD WARS I AND II.

Return to frame 78 and make another choice.

Frame 85

No, though analysis of the concept PHARMACOLOGISTS does indeed imply PROFESSIONALS IN THE FIELD OF PHARMACY, 615.5:331.713 brings up a general rule, *ie* Normally use a special auxiliary in preference to a common auxiliary, if the meaning is the same; and normally use an auxiliary in preference to a coloned code.

Return to frame 77 and make another choice.

Frame 86

325.252 (438) (=924=30) " 1919/1939 " is the appropriate translation of EMIGRATION FROM POLAND OF GERMAN-SPEAKING JEWS DURING
THE PERIOD BETWEEN WORLD WARS I AND II. Note that though =30
must come in the parentheses after (=924 . . .), according to the
examples at the bottom of p 21 the order of most of the other
modifiers could be altered without changing the meaning of the codes
as a whole. Thus 352.252 (=924=30) " 1919/1939 " (438), 325.252
(438) " 1919/1939 " (=924=30), or 325.252 " 1919/1939 " (=924
=30) (438) are all possible with no change of meaning, and do not
exhaust the possibilities. The order given in the answer above, however, is the normal one.

You will have noticed that the index sometimes seems to be un-
reliable, as when it gives ISRAEL, 915.694, which code does not appear
(though it is correct, as constructed out of ' 9 ' and ' (569.4) '), and as
when it gives EMIGRATION, 325.25, which turns out in the schedules
to be either 325.2 or 325.252. The first is likely to be due to a code
having been cut out when the abridgement was done, but the index
entry having been retained unchanged—a not uncommon slip-up
which is occasionally beneficial to the user of the abridged edition.

Proceed to frame 79.

Frame 87

No, 027.7 (05) (05) is not a good choice because it unnecessarily and confusingly forces on the first (05) the sense PERIODICALS a s a s u b j e c t, in defiance of the fact that this sense is more easily available elsewhere.

Return to frame 80 and make another choice.

Frame 88

615.53—05 is a seriously incorrect code produced by a very slight slip-up. The insertion of a colon thus, 615·1:3—05, makes sense, being retranslatable as PHARMACY IN RELATION TO PERSONS IN THE SOCIAL SCIENCES. Perhaps a better code for this case would be 615.1:331-057, retranslatable as PHARMACY IN RELATION TO OCCUPATIONS OF PERSONS IN LABOR ECONOMICS. But this whole periphrasis violates a general rule *i e* : Normally use a special auxiliary in preference to a coloned code. You seem to be too much inclined to accept the first thing that looks likely in the index.

Since the publication of the English third abridged edition, the —05 auxiliary, previously restricted to class 3, has been made available throughout, giving 615.5—05 as the correct translation of PHARMACOLOGISTS.

Return to frame 77 and carefully make another choice.

59

Frame 89

325.252 (=924) " 1919/1939 " is correct in each of its elements; but you have ignored the elements GERMAN-SPEAKING and FROM POLAND.

Return to frame 78.

Frame 90

No, 027.7:05 conveys the subject PERIODICALS IN UNIVERSITY LIBRARIES, but it ignores the form of the material.

Return to frame 80 and make another choice.

Frame 91

No, 548.0:011.001.8 overemphasizes the element EXHAUSTIVE; 011 is appropriate only for bibliographies so exhaustive as to have no such special characteristics or restrictions as being ABOUT CRYSTALLO-GRAPHY. And 015 (73):271.3 overemphasizes the element IN THE UNITED STATES; your code retranslates as RELATION BETWEEN THE FRANCISCAN ORDER AND UNITED STATES NATIONAL BIBLIOGRAPHY.

Return to frame 98 and make another choice.

Frame 92

No, 015:891.58 for [2] disobeys the instruction for specifying 015, although 016:891.58 would make sense to translate A SUBJECT BIBLIO-GRAPHY ON AFGHANI (=Pushtu) LITERATURE. But we are not con-cerned with the belles-lettres of the Pushtu language, but rather with the products of the writers and/or publishers of a particular place.

Return to frame 94 and make another choice.

Frame 93

027.7:05 (05) is the right choice, embodying the distinction between 05 (PERIODICALS as a *subject*) and (05) (PERIODICALS as a *form*). But while it is true that 05 and (05) are parallels—as are also 03, (03); 04, (04); 06, (06); 08, (08)—, these parallels are not absolute, nor can they be extended by the user. For instance, beware of contructing a form-code (07) for NEWSPAPER—even though there is need for it—, or a form-code (09) for MANUSCRIPT, etc. There is, though, one parallelism that is absent, and its absence is n o t due to the fact that something else is in its way, as with 07, (07); 09, (09).

This absent parallelism is for bibliographical works, *i e* (01) as parallel to 01. There seems to be no rational explanation for it, but the fact is that whereas 33:06 and 33 (06) have parallel but easily distinguishable meanings, the two distinct meanings are fused together in each code between 011 and 019. This however is not quite true of 01, which is used for bibliography a s a g e n e r a l s u b j e c t o n l y and never as a form; it is true though for all subdivisions of 01.

Proceed to frame 94.

Frame 94

Choose codes for two documents, [1] *about* THE PROBLEM OF A NATIONAL BIBLIOGRAPHY FOR AFGHANISTAN, and [2] about THE LITERA-TURE OF AFGHANISTAN arranged in that fashion commonly called NATIONAL BIBLIOGRAPHY:

[1] 015 (581)
[2] 015 (581) go to frame 97

[1] 015 (581)
[2] 015:891.58 go to frame 92

[1] 015:958.1
[2] 015 (581) go to frame 100

Frame 95

No, 531.3.001.1 violates the rule of preference given in frame 87. Perhaps you had best re-read frame 77, and then return to frame 101 to make another choice.

Frame 96

No, 548:016.001.8 shows too great a reliance on the index, and that you are not following the golden rule about always checking the schedules before assigning a code: 548 is too general. And 016:271.3 (73) retranslates as A SUBJECT BIBLIOGRAPHY ON AMERICAN FRANCISCANS.

Return to frame 98 and make another choice.

Frame 97

Unfortunately, 015 (581) is the appropriate translation for both [1] and [2], because any other code which means AFGHAN in any sense overspecifies it (*eg* 915.81 its geography, 958.1 its history, 891.58 its belles-lettres, 891.58.07 its philology, =915.8 its language, as form of the book, (=915.8) its ethnic dominance).

A possible solution exists in some cases, as with 016, where a code of the form 33:016 could be taken to mean A SUBJECT BIBLIO-GRAPHY ABOUT ECONOMICS, whereas 016:33 could be taken to mean THE SUBJECT OF SUBJECT BIBLIOGRAPHY AS APPLIED TO ECONOMICS. This is a dangerous solution, though, since each coloned code is officially supposed to be permutable, giving 016:33 as the permuted form of 33:016, and 33:016 as that of 016:33, so that it may be found easily in a catalog under either version.

Proceed to frame 98.

Frame 98

Perhaps a more binding (but less economical) solution of the ambiguity of 011/019 is that, say, 016 can be taken as form, 016.001 as subject.

Choose codes for two documents, [1] about THE POTENTIAL VALUE OF AN EXHAUSTIVE BIBLIOGRAPHY ON CRYSTALLOGRAPHY, and [2] A BIBLIOGRAPHY OF WORKS BY MEMBERS OF THE FRANCISCAN ORDER IN THE UNITED STATES:

[1] 548:016.001.8
[2] 016:271.3 (73) go to frame 96

[1] 548.0:011.001.8
[2] 015 (73):271.3 go to frame 91

[1] 548:016.001.8
[2] 013:271.3 (73) go to frame 101

Frame 99

No, 531.3:001.5 retranslates as THE RELATION OF KINETICS AND GENERAL THEORY OF SCIENCE, which is either too close or too far from THE THEORY OF GENERAL KINETICS to be correct.

Return to frame 101 and make another choice.

Frame 100

No, 015:958.1 for [1] is inappropriate in that the place is given in a way which excludes its geography, etc, by specifying its history. But 015:958.1 would not even translate A SUBJECT BIBLIOGRAPHY ABOUT AFGHAN HISTORY, though 016:958.1 would. But we are not concerned with the history of Afghanistan, nor with subject bibliography, but rather with the products of its writers and/or publishers.

Return to frame 94 and make another choice.

Frame 101

548.0:016.001.8 is the appropriate translation of THE POTENTIAL VALUE OF AN EXHAUSTIVE BIBLIOGRAPHY ON CRYSTALLOGRAPHY; note that the meaning would not change if the code were permuted into 016.001.8:548.0. 013:271.3 (73) is the appropriate translation of A BIBLIOGRAPHY OF WORKS BY MEMBERS OF THE FRANCISCAN ORDER IN THE UNITED STATES; it too permutes, without damage, into 271.3 (73):013. The order in which I have given the elements of each answer merely emphasizes the point that, in [1], 016.001.8 is a subject modifying another subject; and that, in [2], 013 is taken as a form-class which includes any subject to which it is applied.

To return to the rule of preference, and to the fact that it operates only when there is no difference in meaning between the codes that we might use, note that this whole principle equally governs the choice between a common point-of-view auxiliary and any special auxiliary.

Choose a code for a document about THE THEORY OF GENERAL KINETICS:

531.3:001.5 go to frame 99
531.3.01   go to frame 105
531.65.01   go to frame 117
531.3.001.1 go to frame 95

Frame 102

No, if a main-schedule code is written after the subordinate elements of the primary code, as in 8—178 (attempting to translate MUSIC APPLIED TO POETRY), it will have no notational means to maintain itself as a distinct code; or as an 8—1 (6) 78 (attempting to translate MUSIC APPLIED TO AFRICAN POETRY), even if the subordinate element to which it is being joined has its own terminal shell, the added-on main-schedule code will seem to be an extension of the code that began before the initial shell of the subordinate code—as if the (6) were being intercalated into 8—178, whatever that might mean.

Return to frame 171 and make another choice.

Frame 103

No, 875.07:413 is wrong in two ways: first, it uses a cancelled class 4 code, and second, it is redundant, since the 41 in 413 has exactly the same meaning that the .07 has. You have misunderstood the note " As 41 ".

Return to frame 112 to make another choice.

Frame 104

Finally, to reinforce you in the often difficult use of the relocated class 4, choose a code for a document about LINGUISTIC PURITY OF BULGARIAN:

886.7.070.6   go to frame 111
486.7:406   go to frame 106

Frame 105

531.3.01 is the most appropriate translation of THE THEORY OF GENERAL KINETICS, because there is no difference in meaning between it and 531.3.001.1—whereupon the rule of preference in frame 79 takes over. It might be argued that 531.3:001.5 is legitimate, but this would be so only where the book thematically deals with the relation between scientific theory (as a more or less independent subject) and general kinetics—a rather difficult criterion to satisfy, except perhaps for a study in the history of this particular science.

Proceed to frame 112.

Frame 106

You must be kidding! Class 4 is no longer to be used at all except as a model, much less twice in a single code. In any case, the contents of class 4 will be printed as part of class 8 in future editions of UDC, but that does not relieve you of responsibility for being attentive.

The correct answer is accordingly 886.7.070.6, which is constructed on the basis of the language code 886.7, to which is added the PHILO·LOGY special auxiliary .07, and finally the 06 from 406, LINGUISTIC PURITY, repunctuated by the rule of threes.

Read frame 111 as well, and proceed from there.

Frame 107

No, 87:8.07—3 is wrong in three ways: first, it uses the code given in the schedules, 87, as if it were indivisible (but you should know by now that if 47 was divisible, 87 must also be, in a parallel fashion); second, you have made the same mistake as was involved in the second choice given in frame 37; and third, your choice of —3 to represent 413, though in accordance with the instructions at the top of p 58, is disastrous now that class 4 is transferred into class 8, since in class 8 there is an already-established meaning for —3, namely PROSE.

Return to frame 112 and make another choice.

Frame 108

669.45'6'75'76.018.2 is an appropriate translation of THE MALLEABILITY OF PIPE METAL, defined as in the question. This codification avoids cumbersomeness and allows for easy filing under each element as well as under the whole expression. Note that in this case the numerical order of the combined elements is the same as the descending order of the preponderance of those elements—and that this order of preponderance should be followed in preference to mere numerical order, except of course where preponderance is not clearly in evidence.

Proceed to frame 121.

Frame 109

No, 19:944=30 translates THE HISTORY OF PHILOSOPHY AS RELATED TO FRENCH HISTORY, IN GERMAN.

Return to frame 113 and make another choice.

Frame 110

875.073 is the appropriate translation of THE LEXICOGRAPHY OF CLASSICAL GREEK. Note that the instruction " *As* 41 " means that whatever extends 41 can now be used to extend 8.07, but that the instruction at the top of p 58 (by which —3 takes the meaning of 413 when coordinated to a particular language) is invalid because of conflict with 8—3 PROSE.

Proceed to frame 104.

Frame 111

Yes, 886.7.070.6 is the correct translation of LINGUISTIC PURITY OF BULGARIAN. Note that whereas the —1/—8 equivalents to 411/418 are prohibited as getting in the way of 8—1/8—9, there is no similar reason to prohibit —01/—09 as equivalents of 401/409, but that there is no advantage in retention of the —, since in order to mean linguistic as against literary division of the language, the .07 must interpose. Thus the instruction on p 142 might better read :

8	LANGUAGES, LITERATURE AND LINGUISTICS
8.07	PHILOLOGY, LINGUISTICS GENERALLY
8.070	GENERAL QUESTIONS, *As* 40
8.071/.078	GENERAL PHILOLOGY AND LINGUISTICS, *Parallel to* 411/418

It is unfortunate that the transfer of 4 to 8.07, as outlined in these two exercises, is not exactly what is likely to be displayed in the next edition of UDC; but you will be prepared for this eventuality by a thorough comprehension of the underlying principles of UDC.

Proceed to frame 113.

Frame 112

To continue for a little on this important topic of preference between apparently parallel codes, you will now deal with a problem in a class that has been cancelled and its whole function transferred to various other codes. Generally stated class 4 has become subclass 8.07; more specifically 40 has become a special auxiliary, 41 has become 8.07 as such, and the various languages 42/49 have become 82.07/89.07. The note on pp 57-58 posits a parallel between 413.18 and 8.073.18 IDIOMS AND EXPRESSIONS, and between 420:409.3 and 820.07—093 ENGLISH TECHNICAL JARGON. Observe in the first case that 41 simply becomes 8.07, which then continues as before; in the second that 420 becomes 820.07, which continues with a different notation (by 401/409 becoming 01/—09).

Choose a code for a document about THE LEXICOGRAPHY OF CLASSICAL GREEK:

875.07:413	go to frame 103
87:8.07—3	go to frame 107
875.073	go to frame 110
875 (038)	go to frame 114

Frame 113

Another case of a parallelism that must be handled carefully is that between language as form and as subject.

Choose a code for a document IN GERMAN about FRENCH PHILOSOPHY, PRESENTED CHRONOLOGICALLY.

19:944=30	go to frame 109
19 (44)=30	go to frame 116
19 (44):830.07	go to frame 119

Frame 114

No, 875 (038) translates A LEXICON OF CLASSICAL GREEK, rather than
THE LEXICOGRAPHY OF CLASSICAL GREEK.

Return to frame 112 and make another choice.

Frame 115

A device often treated, both officially and unofficially, as a special
auxiliary (because its use is restricted to a small number of classes)
is the apostrophe. Its primary use is for the expression of chemical
synthesis; it is a sort of shorthand way of showing what could more
cumbersomely be shown with the colon. If you had a book about
THE PESSIMISM OF THE NEO-PLATONISTS, the code would be highly
redundant: 141.131 : 141.22; if a code could be used that would stand
for the basic part of the code, such as the apostrophe, 141.131'22
would do the trick. This result is much like that gained by 595.798
(719—08) over 595.798 (719) : 595.798 (1—08), THE WASPS OF THE
UNEXPLORED REGIONS OF LABRADOR; thus the tendency to call the
apostrophe a special auxiliary is increased, even though it does not
(as a special auxiliary does) join a subordinate to a main concept,
but rather joins two concepts of the same sort—almost exactly the
way the colon is defined.

Proceed to frame 118.

3*

Frame 116

19 (44)=30 is the correct translation of FRENCH PHILOSOPHY, PRE-SENTED CHRONOLOGICALLY, IN GERMAN.

The choices presented to you did not, of course, exhaust the possible errors; the most likely would be 19 (44) (091)=30, which is redundant in adding (091) to a code which already means HISTORICAL. Another would be to assume that the element FRENCH called for something other than France as a place; for instance assuming that FRENCH PHILOSOPHY included those works which Leibniz composed in French (he also composed in Latin and German, but it is only to this last as a place that we ordinarily assign him). To take FRENCH to refer to the language rather than the place would lead to a difficult choice between 19=40=30 and 19:840.07=30, but both incorrect.

Proceed to frame 115.

Frame 117

No, the first element of the code, 531.65, was apparently over-hastily chosen from the index because it is the first occurrence of the term KINETIC.

Return to frame 101 and make another choice.

Frame 118

But there is a serious problem about the apostrophe: what it replaces is not clear by principle, but only by instruction. On p 121 you can see it replacing 666.113, while on pp 68-69 it replaces only 546 and 547.

Choose a code for a document about THE MALLEABILITY [a mechanical property] OF PIPE-METAL [a term in the organ-building trade, referring to an alloy of tin, lead, antimony, and bismuth]:

669.45'6'75'76.018.2   go to frame 108
669.45'6'75'76:539.51   go to frame 125
669.45.018.2:669.65.018.2:669.755.018.2:669.765.018.2

go to frame 128

Frame 119

No, 19 (44):830.07 translates THE RELATION BETWEEN FRENCH PHILOSOPHY AND GERMAN PHILOLOGY.

Return to frame 113 and make another choice.

Frame 120

No, 33(82—77)2.1 yields the citation order ECONOMICS—SOUTH AMERICA—ARGENTINA—UNDERDEVELOPED AREAS—PRIVATE FINANCE—BANKING.

Return to frame 165 and make another choice.

Frame 121

The example that you have just seen in frame 117 contained two different kinds of relation between elements of the whole expression: subordination and coordination. Subordination is seen in the relation between 669.4 LEAD ALLOYS and 669.018.2 MALLEABILITY, etc. Coordination is seen between 669.4 and 669.6, between 669.6 and 669.75, etc. Now while in a classed catalog there may be an entry for this document under each named metal, there is a problem of the order in which we should use these elements in the whole single coordinated expression. This problem is also seen in constructing a code consisting of two or more coloned together main-schedule codes.

Proceed to frame 122.

Frame 122

In the example 669.4'6'75'75 the synthesis is truly coordinate; no one element is more essential to the alloy than another (though perhaps present in differing proportions). 141.131 : 141.22 is similarly constructed in so far as ' earlier ' code-elements are written first. But the more common situation is for the various elements of the whole code to stem from widely separate parts of the schedules as a whole; and the rule for their order is, in the most general terms, to put first the substantive and second the epithet. This implies that coloning is not really coordination, and that what modifies comes in the less important (=secondary) position.

Choose a code for a document about THE USE OF ALUMINIUM-BASED PAINTS IN ART:

7.023 : 669.71   go to frame 126
75.023.2 : 667.633.42 : 669.71 go to frame 129
667.6 : 75.023.2   go to frame 134
75.023.2 : 669.71 : 667.633.42 go to frame 136

Frame 123

The problem of determining the order in which you should use codes of the same sort (whether from any one common auxiliary, from any one special auxiliary, or from the main schedules) can be approached in three ways: first, convenience, second, predictability, and third meaning. *Convenience* is what governed the order in either frame 58 or frame 64, namely in terms of the convenience of those who would profit from time aspects being kept together as against those who would profit from place aspects being kept together. *Predictability* is what makes it advisable to obey instructions, as mentioned in frame 129. But *meaning* is the central and ruling point : neither predictability nor convenience can take precedence over accuracy of meaning. It should be thoroughly understood that once a citation order has been established in a given class, in a given library, it is no longer subject to change for mere convenience.

Proceed to frame 124.

Frame 124

A book about TRANSLITERATION OF ARABIC SCRIPT is coded as 003.332
.5.034, one about DIACRITICAL MARKS USED IN ARABIC SCRIPT as
003.332.5.08. Choose codes for two documents, [1] about USE OF
DIACRITICAL MARKS IN TRANSLITERATING ARABIC SCRIPT, and [2]
about TRANSLITERATION OF THE DIACRITICAL MARKS USED IN ARABIC
SCRIPT:

[1] 003.332.5.034.08
[2] 003.332.5.08.034 go to frame 130

[1] 003.08.034.332.5
[2] 003.034.08.332.5 go to frame 127

[1] 003.332.5.08.034
[2] 003.332.5.034.08 go to frame 135

Frame 125

No, 669.45'6'75'76 is correct as translation of PIPE METAL, but : 539.51
as translation of MALLEABILITY shows a forgetfulness that the index
is not always entirely exhaustive, and that auxiliaries are normally to
be preferred to coloned-on main schedule codes.

Return to frame 118 and make another choice.

Frame 126

No; since ART here, in a statement along with PAINT, is usually an overgeneralization for PAINTING, your choice of 7.023 is overgeneral. But another even more serious error has occurred by omission.

Return to frame 122 and make another choice.

Frame 127

No, [1] 003.08.034 and [2] 003.034.08 are all right as translations of the two special auxiliaries as modifications of SCRIPT in general, but the placement of .332.5 makes it a modification of .034 in [1] and of .08 in [2], thus quite preventing it from meaning ARABIC.

Return to frame 124 and make another choice.

Frame 128

No, the mere length and outrageous redundancy of 669.45.018.2 : 669 .65.018.2 : 669.755.018.2 : 669.765.018.2 should tell you that it might be a poor choice—though it is not, strictly speaking, incorrect.

Return to frame 118 and see if another choice conveys the same meaning with less cumbersomeness.

Frame 129

75.023.2 : 667.633.42 : 669.71 is the correct translation of each element of THE USE OF ALUMINIUM-BASED PAINTS IN ART, with each element in the position in the whole as instructed in the schedules. 75.023.2 PAINTING (in terms of the materials involved, namely the coloring material) is to be divided by a colon and 667.6, PAINT AND VARNISH INDUSTRY, and this as further specified in METAL-BASE PAINTS, 667.633.42, is to be divided by a colon and 669, further specified in 669.71, ALUMINIUM. Of course such explicit instructions are not to be expected in the majority of cases.

Proceed to frame 123.

Frame 130

Yes, 003.332.05.034.08 is the appropriate coding for USE OF DIA-
CRITICAL MARKS IN TRANSLITERATING ARABIC SCRIPT and 003.332.5
.08.034 the appropriate coding for TRANSLITERATION OF THE DIA-
CRITICAL MARKS USED IN ARABIC SCRIPT. In this formulation, in the
first example .08 DIACRITICS is made to modify the whole previous
complex 003.332.5.034 ARABIC SCRIPTS—TRANSLITERATIONS; whereas
in the second example .034 TRANSLITERATION is made to modify the
whole previous complex 003.332.5.08 ARABIC SCRIPTS—DIACRITICS.
Thus, to sum up, the varying meaning must be mirrored in a varying
order among the elements of the whole code, and no rules must be
allowed to stand in the way of this meaning.

You have now completed the basic phase of the program. Here are
a few more translations to do as a review, but without the usual
multiple-choice mechanism and explanations.

Proceed to frame 131 for the review problems.

Frame 131

Cover the right-hand column; write the code you construct from
consultation of the schedules on the lines provided for each title-
abstract; slide what you use as a cover down one answer at a time to
check your response.

POPULATION STATISTICS IN TERMS OF AGE AND SEX:	312.9
THE SUFFRAGAN BISHOP IN CHURCH GOVERNMENT:	262.12
PREHISTORIC MAN OF THE COPPER, BRONZE AND IRON AGES:	571 (119.7/8)
THE GEOGRAPHY OF AQUITAINE [south-west France]:	914.47
SEMI-ANNUAL JOURNALS ORIGINATING IN GERMANY (as a subject):	05 (430) " 54—06 "

Proceed to frame 132 to continue the review.

Frame 132

SURGICAL TREATMENT OF PHLEBITIS:

616.14—089

ANIMAL HUSBANDRY BREEDING METHODS
IN THE OCCUPIED ZONES OF FRANCE,
1940-1941:

636.082.4 (44—074)
" 1940/1941 "

A COLLECTION OF ANCIENT LEGAL COM-
MENTARIES ABOUT DIVORCE, WITH THE
COMMENTED-ON TEXTS:

347.627 (095.46)

A COLLECTION OF HISTORICAL SOURCES
ENTITLED " MONUMENTA HISTORIAE MIS-
SIONUM ECCLESIAE ROMANAE ":

266:282 (093)=71

PROCEEDINGS OF A CONFERENCE ABOUT
SYNTACTICAL FACTORS IN LIBRARY
CLASSIFICATION:

025.4:8.076 (063)

CONFERENCE FINANCE:

061.3.047

Proceed to frame 133 to continue the review.

Frame 133

FINANCIAL CONSIDERATIONS IN THE PUB-
LISHING OF PERIODICALS

050.3.003.2

EMIGRATION OF NATIVE INDIANS FROM
TIERRA DEL FUEGO :

325.252 (=98) (828.5)
or
325.252 (828.5=98)

MONTHLY PHILATELIC MAGAZINES IN
GERMAN [as a subject] :

656.835 : 05=30 " 54 "
or
656.835 : 05 " 54 " =30

A MONTHLY MAGAZINE IN GERMAN ABOUT
PHILATELY :

656.835 (05)=30 " 54 "
or
656.835 (05) " 54 " =30

A MONTHLY MAGAZINE IN FRENCH ABOUT
AMERICAN POETRY

820 (73)—1 (05)=40 " 54 "
or
820 (73)—1 (05) " 54 " =40

A BIBLIOGRAPHY OF UNIVERSAL BIBLIO-
GRAPHIES :

016:011

Proceed to the advanced phase frame 137.

Frame 134

No, 667 : 75.023.2 does not follow the rule of thumb given in frame 122, namely that what modifies follows what is modified; also, you have omitted some elements.

Return to frame 122 and make another choice.

Frame 135

No, [1] 003.332.5.08.034 and [2] 003.332.5.034.08 translates the two special auxiliaries in such a way as to make DIACRITICAL MARKS a direct modification of ARABIC SCRIPT in [1], and TRANSLITERATION a direct modification of ARABIC SCRIPT in [2]. But this is not what is implied in the original statements of [1] and [2].

Return to frame 124 and make another choice.

Frame 136

No, 75.023.2.:669.71:667.633.42, though made up of correct elements, does not combine them in an order according to the specific instructions you should have noticed in the schedules.

Return to frame 122 and make another choice.

ADVANCED PHASE

Frame 137

You have now progressed through examples of most of the problems of the use of UDC for which there are either official or unofficial-but-widely-accepted solutions[1]. The solutions hereafter cannot, accordingly, be regarded as being quite as surefooted as those you have seen so far.

You may recall from earlier exercises that a code does not normally begin with an auxiliary. The need for a time period as the major aspect, naturally, will occur seldom; it would be common enough to encounter DANISH MEDIEVAL HISTORY, 948.9 " 04/14 ", or TECHNOLOGY IN MEDIEVAL DENMARK, 62 (489) " 04/14 ". To generalize these topics by the omission of DENMARK is not uncommon either: MEDIEVAL HISTORY [of all places], 94 " 04/14 ", or MEDIEVAL TECHNOLOGY, 62 " 04/14 ". But what about a further generalization by eliminating the elements TECHNOLOGY and HISTORY? You know that " 04/14 " as a main code is prohibited. The solution is implicit in the fact that since no substantive class can serve our purpose, a class must be found which is intended as a summarization of all substantive classes (without being a form-class); this solution is provided in the class THE SCIENCES AND KNOWLEDGE IN GENERAL, OO1.

Proceed to frame 138.

---

[1] One exception to this is the technic called Intercalation, which will be treated in an appendix following the Advanced Phase; this placement is indicative of the problematic status of the technic, even though it is generally sanctioned.

Frame 138

Choose a code for a document about ALL ASPECTS [*ie,* all places and all topics] OF THE MIDDLE AGES, in that form commonly called a BIBLIOGRAPHY:

016: "04/14"	go to frame 141
016:001 "04/14"	go to frame 155
016 "04/14"	go to frame 147

Frame 139

Choose codes for two documents about [1] THE HERRING OF THE DNIEPER DELTA and [2] AGRICULTURAL TOPOGRAPHY OF THE FLOOR OF THE BLACK SEA:

[1] 597.55 (282.247:282.6) [2] 631.47 (262.5.03)	go to frame 142
[1] 639.222 (282.6) [2] 551.4 (262.5.03)	go to frame 148
[1] 597.55 (282.247) [2] 631.47 (26.03)	go to frame 154

Frame 140

You have seen that subordinate facets of a subject are commonly shown by special or common auxiliaries, and that a single code may consist of several such auxiliaries attached to a main-schedule element. In the exercise on TRANSLITERATION and DIACRITICAL MARKS related in various ways to ARABIC SCRIPT you saw that more than one auxiliary of the same sort can be attached to the same primary element. And you have seen that these are special auxiliaries even for the common auxiliaries of space and time.

Often, too, you will encounter documents which will call upon various elements listed within one auxiliary, and you must be prepared to distinguish among the various facets or kinds of element so listed, especially in terms of the order in which to write them. As example take the most notorious: the place auxiliary on pp 12-21. There is the well-known distinction between (3) THE ANCIENT WORLD and (4/9) THE MODERN WORLD, but there is an even stronger difference between (2) PHYSIOGRAPHIC DESIGNATION and (3/9), which last is almost exclusively POLITICAL DESIGNATION. And even within (2) there are concealed sub-facets.

Proceed to frame 139.

Frame 141

No, 016: "04/14" violates the prohibition about using a common auxiliary alone since it could be permuted around the colon into "04/14":016, thus forcing "04/14" to be read as a potentially primary element.

Return to frame 138 and make another choice.

Frame 142

Yes, 597.55 (282.247:282.6) is appropriate for [1], as would also be 597.55 (282.6:282.247). This emphasizes that there are no rules for the construction of non-simple modifiers from the sub-facets of a single auxiliary, so long as the meaning is retained. Nor indeed would 597.55 (282.247) (282.6) be incorrect.

An interesting error that might arise out of a mistaken analogy with (282.243.7) DANUBE (AND ITS DELTA) would be that each river includes its delta; but, even were this the case, a document requiring coding of THE DELTA OF THE DANUBE (without the river as a whole itself) would require specification by adding (282.6) to (282.243.7), either with the colon or in separate parentheses.

Proceed to frame 153.

Frame 143

Choose codes for two documents, [1] about THE RELATION BETWEEN ECONOMICS AND COMMERCE, IN PENNSYLVANIA, and [2] about THE INFLUENCE OF GERMAN LUTHERANISM ON CHURCH MUSIC [in general]:

[1] 33:38 (748)
[2] [783:284.1] (43)   go to frame 151

[1] [33:38] (748)
[2] 783:284.1 (43)   go to frame 157

Frame 144

Yes: as imprecise as it is, this is the best available translation, meaning of course only RELATIONS [wholly unspecified] BETWEEN FRENCH AND VENEZUELAN NEWSPAPER EDITING. The situation does not seem wholly hopeless, however: the FID seems in recent years to be becoming more aware of such deficiencies and to look about for their solution.

Proceed to frame 145.

Frame 145

Another source of error in UDC coding is the fact that subjects in need of special or even of common auxiliaries are lacking them, giving rise to desperate search for something close enough (in words if not in meaning) to substitute.

Choose a code for a document about THE CONSERVATIVE PARTY IN THE CATHOLIC CHURCH SINCE THE SECOND VATICAN COUNCIL [the book is published 1968]:

282 " 1966/1968 ": 165.61 go to frame 152
282 " 1966/1968 ": 262.5　go to frame 160
282 " 1966/1968 ": 165.71 go to frame 156
282 " 1966/1968 ": 329.11 go to frame 163

Frame 146

No, you are getting wild in assuming that the question implied in the title m u s t have an answer, and you then proceed to the most likely supposition, namely that education is better in France, etc.

Return to frame 150 and make another choice.

Frame 147

No, 016 " 04/14 " specifies no subject at all as the subject of a subject bibliography, though it might be taken to translate MEDIEVAL SUBJECT BIBLIOGRAPHIES as a subject. However, you will recall that a convention was suggested that would necessitate the presence of .001 for such a sense, resulting in a code such as 016.001 " 04/14 " to give a truly unambiguous translation of MEDIEVAL SUBJECT BIBLIOGRAPHIES as a subject.

Return to frame 138 and make another choice.

Frame 148

No, 639.222 (282.6) for [1] translates too much in one element : 639.222 is not just HERRING but SEA FISHERIES—HERRING; and (282.6) is DELTAS, but what about THE DNIEPER? For [2], 551.4 is TOPO-GRAPHY, but not AGRICULTURAL TOPOGRAPHY.

Return to frame 139 and make another choice.

Frame 149

There will very often arise cases in which a single modifier modifies more than one of the preceding elements. This after all is perfectly normal in such a code as 33 " 18 " (05), in which (05) modifies the whole previous complex code 33 " 18 ". But what if we substitute 37 for " 18 " and maintain its meaning as COMMERCE by inserting + between it and 33 ECONOMICS. We get 33+37 (05), which surely intends to mean A PERIODICAL ON ECONOMICS AND ON COMMERCE; (05) then does not modify only the element to which it attaches. In fact that would not be possible, because the nasty question would have to arise ' What form does the coverage of economics take?', to which no answer would be possible except ' periodical, of course, if it is found in a periodical about commerce '.

One solution lies in using square brackets to override the normal order of combination, just as in ordinary algebra we give $a.b+c$ if we are adding c to the product of a and b, but $a \cdot [b+c]$ if we want the product of a and the-sum-of-b-and-c.

Proceed to frame 143.

Frame 150

Even in [2] of the previous exercise you can see a problem over the precise meaning of the colon. On p 140 you are told to divide 783 SACRED MUSIC. CHURCH MUSIC. " *By* : 28, *etc.*" This is to be taken as a way of specifying the topic by modifying church-denomination : 783:284.1 means LUTHERAN CHURCH MUSIC. Yet when you need to show the influence (or the comparison, or the detrimental effect, or the belongingness as in the case given) as distinct from each other, there are no means except the colon.

Choose a code for a document examining WHY FRENCH NEWSPAPERS ARE BETTER EDITED THAN VENEZUELAN ONES :

070.4 (44:87)   go to frame 144
070:8.083 (44)+070.4' (87)   go to frame 158
[070.4:37] (44):070.4 (87)   go to frame 146

94

Frame 151

No, 33:38 (748) for [1] is unlike 33+38 (05) in far more than the substitution of : for +, since it could easily be the case that (748) modify either 38 or 33:38. Thus the important substitution is of a place auxiliary for a form auxiliary. Again, then, [783:284.1] (43) for [2] would translate THE RELATION OF CHURCH MUSIC AND LUTHERANISM, IN GERMANY.

Proceed to frame 157.

Frame 152

No, 282 " 1966/1968 ":165.61 is correctly constructed, but shows the very dangerous tendency to classify by your own stance and judgment. Your choice implies IRRATIONALISM IN THE CATHOLIC CHURCH SINCE THE SECOND VATICAN COUNCIL, but this may or may not be what the author thought to be characteristic of the CONSERVATIVE PARTY mentioned.

Return to frame 145 and make another choice.

Frame 153

Further, 631.47 (262.5.03) is the correct translation of [2], avoiding the error of taking TOPOGRAPHY ' straight ', as it were, without adding in AGRICULTURAL; and you will have noticed that the considerably greater ease of constructing a code with a special auxiliary such as (26.03) would recommend the change of (282.6) to such an auxiliary too.

Proceed to frame 149.

Frame 154

No, 597.55 (282.247) is close but not quite close enough, translating THE HERRING OF THE DNIEPER for [1]; similarly, 631.47 (26.03) is very close; it translates AGRICULTURAL TOPOGRAPHY OF THE SEA FLOOR.

Return to frame 139 and make another choice.

Frame 155

Yes, 016:001 " 04/14 " correctly translates A BIBLIOGRAPHY ABOUT ALL ASPECTS OF THE MIDDLE AGES; it avoids the error of coloning the auxiliary " 04/14 " directly to the main-schedule code 016—which would be a use of the colon between codes n o t of the same sort.

Proceed to frame 140.

Frame 156

No, 282 " 1966/1968 ":165.71 is correctly constructed but shows the very dangerous tendency to classify by your own stance and judgment. Your choice implies DOGMATISM IN THE CATHOLIC CHURCH SINCE THE SECOND VATICAN COUNCIL, but this may or may not be what the author thought to be characteristic of the CONSERVATIVE PARTY mentioned—and a classifier with a different stance might well choose for instance : 165.82 REALISM.

Return to frame 145 and make another choice.

4

Frame 157

[33:38] (748) and 783:284.1 (43) are the appropriate translations of [1] THE RELATIONS BETWEEN ECONOMICS AND COMMERCE, IN PENNSYLVANIA and of [2] THE INFLUENCE OF GERMAN LUTHERANISM ON CHURCH MUSIC [in general]. The two exercises differ in that in [1] the modifier IN PENNSYLVANIA applies not only to the two topics, but to their relation; but since the ordinary understanding of these junctures would be, algebraically, $a+b\cdot c$, the brackets are necessary to produce a sub-group out of a and b, prior to the product of that group with $c:$[1]$[a+b]\cdot c$. In [2], on the other hand, brackets are unnecessary and in fact strictly erroneous.

[1] These interpretations can be accepted only provisionally; it is to be hoped that FID may set up more explicit rules, and we must be prepared for just the opposite to what is outlined above—and good argument can be made for such an interpretation.

Proceed to frame 150.

Frame 158

No, you are getting wild in trying to say, in effect, that while French newspapers are edited in a literary manner, Venezuelan ones are not; but you have no warrant for such a conclusion—and there might be a serious difference of opinion as to whether newspaper editing is b e t t e r because more literary.

Return to frame 150 and make another choice.

Frame 159

No; though 37 " 04/14 " (421) 8.4 contains all the essential elements of UNIVERSITIES IN MEDIEVAL LONDON in a meaningful order, the order you have so represented is SOCIAL SCIENCES—EDUCATION—MIDDLE AGES—LONDON—HIGHER—UNIVERSITIES.

Return to frame 167 and make another choice.

Frame 160

No, 282 " 1966/1968 ":262.5 translates THE INFLUENCE OF THE CHURCH COUNCILS ON THE CATHOLIC CHURCH SINCE THE SECOND VATICAN COUNCIL, but does not mention THE CONSERVATIVE PARTY. (Note that even non-decimal extension of 262.5 to 262.5V2 or 262.5 " 1962/1965 " is not sufficient to specify the influenced sector of the Church.)

This however is probably the closest you will be able to get (though, as with all living classifications, the growing presence of such problem-documents forces extensions and corrections, which are of course not to be found in your 1961 schedules).

Therefore, return to frame 145 and check out the erroneous frames that you have not looked at up to now and then proceed to frame 161.

APPENDIX ON INTERCALATION

Frame 161

In the basic phase and the advanced phase you have come to grips with the problems, techniques, and tentative solutions that arise from use of UDC. One technique though has been omitted up to now: intercalation.

The purpose of intercalation is to change citation order. The codes 342.5 (492) AUTHORITIES. POWERS—NETHERLANDS, 342.51 (492) EXECUTIVE POWER—NETHERLANDS, and 342.518 (492) CABINET—NETHERLANDS might not appeal to a Netherlands classifier interested in keeping all such levels of material on his country together. This desire can be accomplished simply by moving all the parenthesized elements left to whatever position is desired. The place code can be stabilized to follow 342.5, 342, 34 or even 3. The further over it is moved, the more strongly is NETHERLANDS collocated within class 3.

Proceed to frame 167.

Frame 162

No, if a main-schedule code is coloned in wherever needed, as in 8:78—1 (attempting to translate MUSIC APPLIED TO POETRY), the subordinate of the primary code will seem to be attached to the coloned-in main-schedule code.

Return to frame 171 and make another choice.

Frame 163

No, most decidedly not: 282 " 1966/1968 " is correct (after all, it is an element in each of the four possible choices), but : 329.11 brings in a context that cannot but invalidate the translation you are attempting, since 32 means POLITICAL PARTIES in the purely civil sense. Your translation really means THE [unspecified] RELATION BETWEEN THE CATHOLIC CHURCH SINCE THE SECOND VATICAN COUNCIL AND CONSERVATIVE POLITICAL PARTIES [throughout the world]; but if this is the desired meaning (for a different document, that is), it would be better conveyed with the time-auxiliary at the end, modifying both previous elements.

Proceed to frame 161, where the appendix on intercalation begins.

Frame 164

Yes, 37 (421) " 04/14 " 8.4 not only translates all the essential elements of UNIVERSITIES IN MEDIEVAL LONDON, but also displays them in the citation order requested in frame 167.

The answer in frame 166, 378 " 04/14 " 4 (421) is of interest in that the decimal point that is to be found in the other answers is absent. Though this is wholly in keeping with the fact that the decimal point carries no meaning except when it precedes the digit ' o ', it seems at least potentially capable of causing misunderstanding, as if it were the main class 4 that follows " 04/14 ". But a far more serious danger is that such flexibility will lead to a total breakdown of predictability —since all the answers to frame 167 are correct, each representing a different citation order.

Note that any code that carries its own shell, a symbol that opens and closes the code, can easily be intercalated—in this case the " 04/14 ".

Proceed to frame 165.

Frame 165

As you can see from the example in frames 161 and 167, any code that carries along its own shell—in the form of parentheses or quotes —is easy to intercalate. But what about other codes? The difficulty is that there would be nothing to show the terminus of $=30$ if we wanted to arrange all our sociology entries by the language of the documents. If we start with 301.16$=$30, SOCIAL SCIENCES—SOCIOLOGY —SOCIAL RELATIONS—IN GERMAN, a change to SOCIAL SCIENCES— SOCIOLOGY—IN GERMAN—SOCIAL RELATIONS would give 301$=$3016. Retention of the normal decimal point here might seem to solve the problem—301$=$30.16—but a change to SOCIAL SCIENCES—IN GERMAN—SOCIOLOGY—SOCIAL RELATIONS would then seem doomed to 30$=$301.16 and total confusion, were it not for the availability of square brackets as *ad hoc* shells for codes without them, as in 30[$=$30]1.16.

Choose a code for a document about BANKING IN THE UNDERDEVEL-OPED AREAS OF ARGENTINA, displaying the citation order ECONOMICS —SOUTH AMERICA—UNDERDEVELOPED AREAS—ARGENTINA—PRIVATE FINANCE—BANKING:

33 (8[$-$77]2)2.1 go to frame 171
33 (82$-$77)2.1   go to frame 120
33 (8$-$772)2.1   go to frame 168

Frame 166

No; though 378 " 04/14 " 4 (421) contains all the essential elements of UNIVERSITIES IN MEDIEVAL LONDON in a meaningful order, the order you have so represented is SOCIAL SCIENCES—EDUCATION—HIGHER—MIDDLE AGES—UNIVERSITIES—LONDON.

Return to frame 167 and make another choice.

Frame 167

For instance, 342.518 (492) has the citation order

3	SOCIAL SCIENCES.
34	JURISPRUDENCE. LAW. LEGISLATION.
342	PUBLIC LAW. CONSTITUTIONAL LAW.
342.5	AUTHORITIES. POWERS.
342.51	EXECUTIVE POWER.
342.518	CABINET. COUNCIL OF MINISTERS.
342.518 (492)	NETHERLANDS.

and this order can be changed, for instance, to

3	SOCIAL SCIENCES.
34	JURISPRUDENCE. . . .
34 (492)	NETHERLANDS.
34 (492)2	PUBLIC LAW. . . .
34 (492)2.5	AUTHORITIES. . . .
34 (492)2.51	EXECUTIVE POWER.
34 (492)2.518	CABINET. . . .

Choose a code for a document about UNIVERSITIES IN MEDIEVAL LONDON, displaying the citation order SOCIAL SCIENCES—EDUCATION —LONDON—MIDDLE AGES—HIGHER—UNIVERSITIES :

37 " 04/14 " (421) 8.4   go to frame 159
378 " 04/14 " 4 (421)   go to frame 166
37 (421) " 04/14 " 8.4   go to frame 164

Frame 168

No, 33 (8—722) 2.1 is open to a serious misunderstanding, since there is no way to tell where the area-characteristic (. . . —77 . . .) ends, and that the digit ' 2 ' is an extension of the digit ' 8 ' in (82).

Return to frame 165 and make another choice.

Frame 169

The illogicality of the instruction (to intercalate a main-schedule code into the centre of a total code by bracketing it in wherever needed) occurs when the codes which are grouped together in the second interpretation on frame 170 must stand in an explicit relation to some code external to them, as in [54+66.0] (469) CHEMISTRY AND CHEMICAL ENGINEERING IN PORTUGAL, where the parentheses show explicitly that what they contain is a place modification subordinate to the main-schedule codes. Again, if such a complex as 22/28:301.007.1 SOCIOLOGISTS OF THE CHRISTIAN RELIGION is to be joined to another main-schedule code, it needs a colon between its *ad hoc* shell and that other code, as in [22/28:301.007.1]:174 PROFESSIONAL ETHICS OF . . .

Of course, when one main-schedule code is intercalated into another, the colon cannot stand outside the brackets, lest it govern (mistakenly) the terminal modifier of the primary element, as in 8:[78]−1 (which could then read, minus the intercalated code, as 8:−1, a violation of the rule for use of the colon only between codes of the same sort); it must then stand inside the brackets, as in 8[:78]−1, as distinct from 8[+78]−1 POETRY and MUSIC.

Proceed to frame 172.

Frame 170

According to the instructions at the top of p 11 (but, unfortunately, none too logically), a main-schedule code is to be intercalated into the centre of a total code by being bracketed in wherever needed as in 8[78]—1 (translating MUSIC APPLIED TO POETRY).

You will notice, in summary, first, that the brackets may be used to provide an *ad hoc* shell to allow intercalation of codes without their own shells; and second, that they can be used to group elements of a total code so as to override the usual order of combination (*cf* frame 149). Even a third use is proposed on p 11 : that brackets can enclose a main-schedule code which stands in a purely subordinate relation to another main-schedule code; but this usage has recently been taken over by the double colon (no exercises are given for this new device).

Proceed to frame 169.

Frame 171

Yes, 33 (8[—77]2)2.1 translates BANKING IN THE UNDERDEVELOPED AREAS OF ARGENTINA, in a citation order that places area-characteristics immediately after continent-codes, and does so in a fashion that prevents confusion—as in (8—772)—between the area-characteristic code and the digit ' 2 ' which extends the mere place code (8) into (82).

You have seen the use of the shelled codes for intercalation, and how to create an *ad hoc* shell for a code without one. The purpose of intercalation is to change the normal citation order (a library for international economic and social problems might need area-characteristics kept more close together than mere places), but one of the commonest codes to need a changed citation order is a main-schedule code.

How is a main-schedule code intercalated into the centre of a total code?

by being simply written after the subordinate elements of the primary code :   go to frame 102
by being coloned in wherever needed :   go to frame 162
by being bracketed in wherever needed :   go to frame 170.

Frame 172

The only conclusion is that the technique of intercalation is so dangerously ambiguous, at least in regard to main-schedule codes, as to be unsafe as the basis for exercises; it is so inclined to lead to a perilous unpredictability when used with self-shelled auxiliaries and *ad hoc*-shelled bracketed auxiliaries, that it is best avoided except in organizations capable of developing and enforcing rules of citation order which necessitate it (as in such a library as is mentioned in frame 171).

Now you have completed the program and are (hopefully) in a position to begin to learn about UDC by practice and by speculative investigation. You have progressed from simple problems to those involving system difficulties (as when several modifiers are to be attached to a compound or complex main concept), as well as semantic difficulties (as when unfamiliar but perhaps simple concepts are involved); and you have had the opportunity to see how a synthetic classification is able to cope with such problems—and you have only become acquainted with the abridged edition so far.

FROM NOW ON IT IS UP TO YOU.

CONCEPT INDEX